COPS AREN'T SUCH BAD GUYS

by Paul Brakke

Author of *American Justice*? and *The Price of Justice in America*

COPS AREN'T SUCH BAD GUYS

Copyright © 2017 by Paul Brakke

All rights reserved. No part of this book may be used or reproduced by any means, graphic, electronic, or mechanical, including photocopying, recording, taping or by any information storage retrieval system without the written permission of the author except in the case of brief quotations embodied in critical articles and reviews.

ACKNOWLEDGMENTS

I wanted to extend my thanks to Gini Graham Scott for conducting the interview with Georgia attorney Lance LoRusso, who specializes in representing cops in fatality cases. She also assisted in writing the chapters of the book.

TABLE OF CONTENTS

CHAPTER 1: COPS AND FATAL SHOOTINGS 7
   What the Stats Show about Police Killings 8
   The Latest Trends 10
   What's the Solution? 12

CHAPTER 2: HOW MISINFORMATION LEADS TO ANGER AGAINST COPS AND THE SYSTEM 15
   The Major Sources of Misinformation 15
   Misunderstandings about Use of Force 17
   Misunderstandings about the Need for Quick Action 19

CHAPTER 3: THE EXTENSIVE HEARINGS AFTER A FATAL SHOOTING 23
   The Four Types of Hearings 23
   The Administrative Review 25
   The Criminal Investigation and Prosecutorial Review 25
   The Criminal Trial 27
   The Civil Litigation 29
   The High Financial and Psychological Costs 29

CHAPTER 4: THE ROLE OF THE MEDIA IN PROMOTING VIOLENCE IN POLICE FATALITIES 31
   How the Media Can Spread a False Story 31
   How the Police Should Respond to False Information 33
   Balancing Out What's True and False 35
   The Killings of Black Males and the Police 36
   How to Correct the Misperceptions 38

ABOUT THE AUTHOR 41

CHAPTER 1: COPS AND FATAL SHOOTINGS

Today, there is an apparent uptick in the number of fatal shootings of citizens by cops. However, this impression is not accurate, since publicity about individual shootings has been fanned by the media and the Black Lives Matter movement. Moreover, the perception is that the cops have wantonly engaged in these killings, using racial profiling to target African-Americans, who are the major victims in these shootings. Subsequently, after the officers involved have been cleared of wrongdoing as a result of administrative hearings and trials, the perception is that the criminal justice system is corrupt in letting guilty officers off because the system is wrongly protecting them. The result has been the further impression that the exoneration of these officers reflects a system-wide bias against African-Americans, which has fueled further protests supporting the Black Lives Matter movement and has contributed to the growing divisiveness in U.S. society today.

However, these impressions and perceptions are misleading, because they don't take into account the difficulties which the police face. I want to examine this issue of what happens when a police officer is involved in a fatal shooting in this next series of blogs, drawing on recent research and an extensive interview with Lance LoRusso, an attorney in Georgia, who specializes in representing police officers in administrative, criminal, and civil hearings. He has written two books about fatal shootings by cops: *When Cops Kill*[1] and *Blue News*[2]. In the first of these books, he describes at length the various procedures that cops go through after they kill a citizen in the course of duty, and in the second book, he looks at the role of the media in writing about what the police do – and how the media often get it wrong.

What the Stats Show about Police Killings

First, I want to provide a more accurate description of the number of citizens killed by police officers each year, as well as the number of police killed on duty, which provides a broader context for what is really going on. These numbers put the lie to the first perception that the bulk of these deaths are caused by out-of-control police officers who are racially biased against African-Americans, so they are more likely to shoot them.

It is actually very difficult to get an accurate picture of these statistics, since the data collected by the Department of Justice's new system to determine the number of homicides by police shows over twice the rates reported by the FBI, according the a report by the *Guardian*[3].

Similarly, the accounts of the number of police killed each year can be misleading, because the number of officers has increased dramatically in the United States, as reported in a BBC

---

[1] Lance LoRusso, *When Cops Kill,* Blue Line Lawyer, 2013.
[2] Lance LoRusso, *Blue News*, Blue Line Lawyer, 2016.
[3] John Swayne and Ciara McCarthy, "Killings by US Police Logged at Twice the Previous Rate Under New Federal Program," December 15, 2016. https://www.theguardian.com/us-news/2016/dec/15/us-police-killings-department-of-justice-program

article: "U.S. Police Shootings: How Many Die Each Year?"[4] The article reports that the numbers of police killed have actually been declining since 1975. Then, too, the media focus on a few big incidents, such as the series of deaths by anti-police snipers and terrorists. Such stories give the impression that the police are under siege, while other stories highlight some of the latest killings by police to suggest that the police are targeting more victims.

So what is the most accurate picture? According to the National Law Enforcement Officers Memorial Fund, in 2015, 123 officers died in the line of duty, a number generally in line with previous years, and in the last four years, 40-50 officers were "shot, stabbed, strangled or beaten to death each year." In fact, before the Dallas shootings in which a gunman killed five officers in response to the killing of two black men by police officers in

---

[4] BBC News, "U.S. Police Shootings: How Many Die Each Year?" July 18, 2016. http://www.bbc.com/news/magazine-36826297

Baton Rouge, the number of police deaths was actually down 12 percent for the same time as the previous year.[5]   But after that, the number of police officers killed by firearms was up 17 percent. So overall more cops are not being killed in the line of duty, although more of those being killed may be the victims of targeted killings.

At the same time, it would seem there really has been an increase in the number of homicides by police, in part due to a better count of killings and the use of force by police officers. This increase has occurred since the unrest in Ferguson, Missouri, after the August 2014 shooting of Michael Brown led to protests and riots in the town and across the U.S. Before that, the annual count of homicides by the police reported by the FBI depended on police chiefs voluntarily submitting their numbers. After that, the U.S. Department of Justice reported nearly twice as many killings, approximately 1080 deaths for all of 2015.[6] As of December 15, 2016, the Guardian recorded 1025 deaths, which is approximately the same as 2015. Since 2000, all sources other than the FBI report a rising trend of killings by police.[7] The FBI relies on reports from police departments, but many departments don't provide this information, so the FBI counts are much less than those of the Department of Justice.

The Latest Trends

Thus, there has been no significant increase in the number of police killed over the last few years, although the statistics do seem to support the popular perception, fueled by the media, that

---

[5] Lisa Desjardins, "The History of U.S. Police Deaths in the Line of Duty," PBS News Hour, July 8, 2016, (http://www.pbs.org/newshour/rundown/the-history-of-u-s-police-deaths-in-the-line-of-duty

[6] John Swayne and Ciara McCarthy, "Killings by US Police Logged at Twice the Previous Rate Under New Federal Program."

[7] Daniel Beir, "How Many Americans Do the Cops Kill Each Year, " *Newsweek*, July 16, 2016, http://www.newsweek.com/how-many-americans-do-cops-kill-each-year-480712

there have been more killings of citizens by the police. A reason for this, according to LoRusso, is that there has been a growing tendency for citizens to resist the authority of the police, which leads to escalating conflict in police-citizen encounters. As he pointed out, "More people engage in confrontations with the law in which suspects escalate the situation. They won't put up their hands, they won't respond to an officer's commands, or they fight back, like in the situation with Eric Garner."

Then, too, LoRusso observed that the "war on the police is real," in describing some of the situations in which officers are fired upon and attacked by individuals from different circumstances, both from the inner city and rural environments. To a great extent, these situations are due to ambushes which are actually rare occurrences – only 21 in 2015, but they have been a key factor in increasing fear among the police and the call for more law and order by fearful citizens. For instance, he pointed out how in recent cases in his own state of Georgia, seven police officers were shot and two were killed. He also observed that many of these attacks came from "people who are already in the criminal justice system," and many of these people were involved in the violence of the drug trade or in other violent encounters on the street. Additionally, this hostility to the police would seem to be not only from Black Lives Matter members and other activists, since some protests have included not only blacks but other groups. For example, LoRusso described how in one protest in Texas, a mix of individuals from different racial groups chanted "Dead cops now," while in another case, a group of Black Panthers assembled who were calling for the death of cops.

Unfortunately, the media help to give voice to these protests and calls for the death of cops, which contributes to fueling further protests and hostility to the police. This hostility then exacerbates the confrontations when the police try to make an arrest, which can lead to an increase in both killings by police and further citizen attacks on the police.

What's the Solution?

Yet the answer isn't to reduce the police presence in communities where these confrontations have occurred, since as LoRusso observed, most residents in the inner cities, where there is a high level of crime, want police protection for themselves. They don't want the police to retreat in the face of attacks by criminals and terrorists, as they have done recently in Chicago despite a real escalation of gang-related murders.

So what is the answer? How do we repair the growing divide between the police and many citizens, especially in high-crime inner city communities? I'll discuss some possibilities in future blogs.

CHAPTER 2: HOW MISINFORMATION LEADS TO ANGER AGAINST COPS AND THE SYSTEM

Since the shooting of Michael Brown in Ferguson, Missouri by the police in 2014, there has been a growing anger against the police, especially after several more police shootings and other arrest incidents led to deaths. The resulting protests and riots have, in turn, triggered even more anger, much of it fueled by the media which have played up these incidents. More and more venom has been heaped on the police, who are viewed by some as out-of-control racist killers, leading to even more attacks on them and on the criminal justice system as a corrupt enabler. A common trigger for these citizen and media attacks is when the police investigations lead to clearing the police officer charged with a fatal homicide.

The Major Sources of Misinformation

However, a major reason for this anger and the resulting upheavals is the misinformation that occurs in two key ways. According to an interview with Lance LoRusso, an attorney in Georgia who specializes in representing police officers in fatality incidents and has written two books on this topic: *When Cops Kill* and *Blue News,* there are two major sources of misinformation. One occurs because citizens don't understand the police use of force guidelines, whereby the police are trained on when they can use deadly force. In addition, citizens don't understand the careful assessment of a homicide committed by a police officer, which occurs at four levels within the criminal justice system – the administrative internal review process, the criminal investigation by the police, the prosecutor's decision to charge or not charge a crime, and the courts if a trial occurs. If citizens understood this process, they would recognize that in most cases, the police officer is not at fault in using his or her gun for self-defense in these difficult confrontations where the officer reasonably believes his or her life or that of someone else is under immediate threat and shoots for that reason.

Another source of this misunderstanding is the misinformation that gets out through the social media without being quickly corrected. Frequently, witnesses or activists put out false information about what actually happened to suggest that the police officer wasn't under threat, and this false information becomes the narrative that furthers hostility to the police and the system. I'll talk about these false narratives leading to violence in another blog. Here I want to focus on the misunderstandings about the use of force and the administrative procedures affecting any police-citizen encounters that result in citizen fatalities. According to LoRusso, these violent confrontations have increased in recent years due to increased citizen resistance to the police in these encounters, which has contributed to these fatalities. Also, citizens commonly misunderstand how these violent encounters trigger use of force guidelines that provide that officers can shoot the citizens resisting them in order to protect themselves.

Misunderstandings about Use of Force

The basic policy underlying the use of force is that an officer can use deadly force when he perceives his own life or that of another party under his protection is in danger of harm from the perpetrator. As Lance LoRusso explains in *When Cops Kill*, the use of deadly force in law enforcement occurs under three circumstances where it is considered necessary – to effect an arrest, to protect the law enforcement officer (also called an LEO), and to protect a third person. Accordingly, whenever there is a death due to the actions of a police officer, the analysis to determine if the officer acted appropriately begins by looking at whether the force was to "maintain order, effect an arrest, defend the LEO from attack, or defend a third party."[8]

Then, a further consideration is what the state statute permits, since nearly every state has a statute that justifies the use of force by LEOs. For example, the statute in Georgia, where LoRusso works, states this:

---

[8] LoRusso, *When Cops Kill, p. 19.*

> "Sheriffs and peace officers…may use deadly force to apprehend a suspected felon only when the officer reasonably believes that the suspect possesses a deadly weapon or any object, device, or instrument which, when used offensively against a person, is likely to or actually does result in serious bodily injury; when the officer reasonably believes that the suspect poses an immediate threat of physical violence to the officer or others; or when there is probable cause to believe that the suspect has committed a crime involving the infliction or threatened infliction of serious physical harm."[9]

In addition, the code permits sheriffs or peace officers to use any reasonable nondeadly force as necessary to apprehend and arrest a suspected felon or misdemeanant, although if the suspect resists and escalates the arrest into a confrontation where the officer fears for his life, that officer has the authority to use deadly force. At the same time, the officer has the burden of proving that his or her actions were justified in a use of force analysis, which leaves open the door to being prosecuted for the inappropriate use of force. This is why some of these killings by the police have led to prosecutions, especially when there is citizen and media pressure to call the officer to account. A prosecution can even occur when an initial administrative review has found that the officer has acted appropriately within these guidelines. Unfortunately, regardless of the fact that the media seek to inform the public swiftly about events, while the justice system seeks to give the police the same deliberate protections under the law as other citizens, the accused cop's career and finances are seriously undermined, even if he or she is found innocent.

---

[9] Ibid., pp. 19-20.

One source of misunderstanding about the use of force is what is a reasonable belief. In general, citizens don't understand that these judgments about whether the officer acted reasonably are based on what a law enforcement officer would reasonably believe is a real danger from the suspect rather than what an average citizen would believe. These beliefs can differ because the officer has a truer understanding of the nature of the danger than the average person, due to the officer experiencing many months of training on when to use deadly force in response to a perception of danger. By contrast, the average citizen may not recognize the danger, whereas the officer does.

For example, in an interview, LoRusso pointed out how quickly a suspect can fire a gun or come at an officer with a knife, and how it can be difficult for an officer to accurately distinguish whether the suspect has a gun or not in a low light situation, which is when most citizen-police encounters occur. Thus, in a common scenario, it might be difficult to determine whether the suspect is holding a gun which could be deadly or a cell phone which is not. So which is it? Upon seeing the potential danger, the officer has only moments in which to react by using deadly force to protect himself, because if he hesitates and is wrong, he will die.

Misunderstandings about the Need for Quick Action

Generally, citizens don't understand this need for quick action, when they later claim the officer shouldn't have shot, because the suspect only had a toy gun or a cell phone. But at the time, the officer didn't know, and when the suspect didn't respond to his command to immediately put up his hands, the officer felt his or her life at risk. Accordingly, in such a situation, the officer is justified to shoot, though many citizens don't understand why he or she had the right to do so.

Another problem is that citizens don't understand how quickly a suspect's attack can turn deadly, which is another reason an officer might respond with deadly force rather than taking the risk that the suspect will shoot or charge with a knife. For example, as LoRusso explained, a person with a gun in his belt can fire that gun in 0.2 seconds by just pointing and shooting it. Then, it takes 2.5 seconds for each follow-up shot. By contrast, he claims that if an officer tries to pull his gun out of his holster to shoot, it takes about 7.6 to 8.3 seconds, which means that if the officer waits to see if the suspect will fire, he will be shot and perhaps killed.

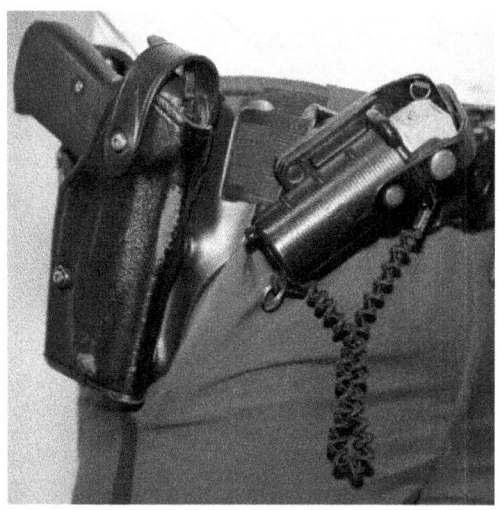

So the officer will normally already have his gun drawn when confronted by a potentially dangerous situation, so he or she can shoot immediately. Otherwise the person with the gun can shoot the officer three times before the officer is able to shoot back. Under the circumstances, in a low-light situation, an officer has a fraction of a second to determine whether something the suspect is holding is a weapon or a cell phone, and so is reasonably permitted to shoot to kill.

Few citizens go through a Citizen's Police Academy class where they might recognize how a delay in responding to a potentially deadly incident could be disastrous. In such a class, they experience a training simulator in which they are presented with a series of potentially deadly encounters, where the suspect has a gun, knife, or object that could be a weapon or cell phone.

In the simulation, the citizen has a laser gun and can shoot at any time, resulting in a hit or miss depending on how well he or she shoots. In various scenarios, the citizen acting as a police officer tells the suspect he or she is under arrest, asks the suspect to put down a weapon, hold up his hands, or sees the suspect threaten a hostage. Then, as the suspect reacts in various ways, the citizen/officer can shoot or not. In a common scenario, the citizen/officer doesn't respond quickly enough or shoots and misses, and ends up dead. It is a dramatic demonstration of how quickly an officer has to react in such a confrontation to save his or her own life or that of another person who is threatened by the suspect.

Given the realities of these potentially deadly encounters, in training programs around the United States, officers are trained on how to respond quickly and intuitively, without thinking about what to do, in order to reasonably make these split second decisions. Accordingly, it is important to judge these actions from the perspective of a reasonable law enforcement officer, not from the safety of a judge's chambers, as LoRusso pointed out. By the same token, an individual with a knife can charge an officer in a few seconds, so even if the officer sees a person threatening with a knife, that can be just as deadly, if he or she doesn't already have a gun drawn and shoots first.

    Unfortunately, the average citizen doesn't understand this need for the officer to respond almost instantaneously under usually low-light conditions, when a suspect is resisting and might be armed with a gun or a knife. So the citizen might readily claim an officer unjustly killed the victim and use that to fuel a protest movement to seek justice for the victim, as has occurred after numerous recent deaths by cops from Ferguson, Missouri to Baton Rouge, Louisiana. But in most of these cases, the officer was justified to shoot, as later determined through a series of hearings about the case. And that is what I'll discuss in the next blog -- how the administration of justice works, since this is another area of misunderstanding leading many citizens to conclude that these hearings are fixed by a corrupt criminal justice system, when that is not true.

CHAPTER 3: THE EXTENSIVE HEARINGS AFTER A FATAL SHOOTING

Citizens commonly think that the police are getting off easy after an officer shoots a citizen and is judged to not be at fault. While they attribute this result to a biased criminal justice system that is predisposed to judge the officer not guilty or not responsible, this perception is not true. As previously noted, an officer is judged based on his or her training and adherence to use of force principles, and in almost all of these shootings, the officer is judged to have followed these policies and to have only used deadly force when he or she felt a risk to him or herself or to a third party.

Not only do citizens generally not understand these policies, they do not understand the many hearings which a police officer has to undergo after such a shooting. At these hearings, the officer is judged again and again as to whether he or she followed the use of force principles and really felt that he or she or a third party was at risk of injury or death under the circumstances. Moreover, as comes out at these hearings, the citizens' original perception and beliefs about the incident are often wrong, because they are based on incorrect facts that get circulated by social media and are later reported as true by the mainstream media. But once the evidence of what actually happened is in, the officer's report about what happened becomes justified, and the false information circulating about the incident is generally refuted.

The Four Types of Hearings

As Lance LoRusso, a Georgia attorney who specializes in representing police officers involved in fatal shootings, points out, after a shooting, a police officer actually goes through four levels of hearing within the criminal justice system. These four levels of hearings include the following, which LoRusso also discusses in his book *When Cops Kill*: an administrative internal affairs hearings, a criminal investigation by the police, a decision by the prosecutor as to whether to charge a complaint or not, and a trial if the complaint is charged.

While the officer is still at the scene of the incident, as LoRusso writes in *When Cops Kill,* he or she should "provide information to investigators to help identify a suspect who has left the scene to aid in his capture and help secure medical treatment if he is injured." (p. 32) At this point, the officer also has to turn over his weapon and any other equipment used during the encounter.

However, immediately after the incident, the officer will often recall very little of what happened and will have difficulty answering questions or providing "coherent and complete answers," due to the stress of what happened. So to ordinary citizens and activists it may appear that the officer is trying to cover up or change the narrative of what really occurred, but in fact, the officer is often in something of a state of shock and may not know what occurred. This state of shock is common when the officer is literally staring the potential for death in the face.

The Administrative Review

Almost immediately after the fatal incident, the first review is an administrative review, commonly handled by the police department's Internal Affairs Division, which looks at whether the officer correctly followed the department's use of force procedures, which were established through state law.

In some jurisdictions there also may be a citizens' review panel to look at the incident and make recommendations, usually to the police Internal Affairs Division, as to whether a crime occurred. In some cities, the review board may announce its decision publicly. While there is some controversy about the need for and propriety of such panels, the concept is firmly established in the United States, as LoRusso notes. Commonly, the members of these panels include community leaders, politicians, the media, and advocates. In some communities, such as Oakland, California, which has highly divisive responses to the police, the review panel has a strong anti-police leaning, which has led to extensive disputes with the police union and other community members who are more supportive of the police.

The Criminal Investigation and Prosecutorial Review

The second type of review is conducted by criminal investigators from the police department. They descend on the scene, secure it, and begin processing the evidence. Commonly, they wait several days to interview the police officer who killed the suspect, because they are aware the officer is in a highly emotional shocked state. As LoRusso notes in *When Cops Kill*, as a general rule, federal agents do not speak with anyone for at least seventy hours following a killing."[10] When this interview occurs, officers have the same rights as an ordinary citizen, in that they can ask to have an attorney present during questioning to observe the process,

---

[10] LoRusso, *When Cops Kill*, p. 35.

advise them about the questions asked and their response to them, and whether to continue the interview.[11]

Commonly, during the interview, officers will be asked to draw a diagram of the scene and indicate where they were standing, their position relative to the suspect, and how many times they fired their gun. The officer often may not recall this information and so cannot answer, because, as LoRusso points out, he or she has experienced auditory exclusion before using this force. This auditory exclusion is a psychological reaction in response to intense stress that limits what a person hears.[12] Thus, though an average citizen or activist might perceive that the officer is lying or distorting what happened, actually this lack of response is due to the officer truly not recalling what happened.

If the criminal investigators find some evidence that suggests the shooting could be a crime, the third level of investigation of the fatal incident is a prosecutorial review. At this stage, the prosecutor looks at the evidence collected by the criminal investigators to determine if there is sufficient evidence to warrant a criminal trial. Alternatively, some prosecutors may turn to a grand jury or seek to have a federal inquiry into what occurred. These grand juries are made up of individuals in the community who are selected by a court to decide if it is appropriate for the government to prosecute someone suspected of a crime. If the jurors decide that the case warrants prosecution, they will issue an indictment, after which the prosecutors will proceed. In the event that prosecutors look to the federal government for assistance, then federal prosecutors in the U.S. Department of Justice will review the case and decide if it merits prosecution. A reason that prosecutors might look to a grand jury or federal authorities is if the case has been widely publicized or has become controversial, so that opposing sides have different views as to whether a suspect is guilty or not. In this way, the prosecutor can be viewed as being

---

[11] Ibid., p. 39.
[12] Ibid., pp. 40-41.

more neutral in assessing the case, rather than appear to be taking sides based on popular opinion.

The Criminal Trial

Should there then be sufficient grounds for a criminal prosecution, the fourth stage is having a criminal trial, which is what happened in some high-profile cases.

For example, in Baltimore, four officers were tried when Freddie Gray suffered from injuries in the back of a police van while he was being taken to jail after an arrest. There was also a trial in the Michael Brown case in Ferguson, Missouri, where Officer Darren Wilson was tried for allegedly shooting Brown in the back. In still another widely publicized case, Eric Garner died in Staten Island after an officer put him in a chokehold while he was resisting arrest. In these and many other cases, the officers were found not guilty, despite the widespread public belief that the officers were guilty and the criminal justice system was corrupt because they were set free.

However, this is where the public perception of a case can differ from the weight of the evidence and the standards of proof of intent in a criminal trial. For example, in the Freddie Gray case, a reason for the not-guilty verdict was the lack of the officers' intent in causing Gray's death, though their negligence in not securing him properly in the back of the van provided justification for a civil trial and a verdict in favor of the Gray family.

In the Wilson case, there was extensive evidence that countered the popular narrative that Wilson shot Brown in the back while Brown was running away. In fact, as LoRusso noted, the evidence showed that Brown struggled with Wilson in his police car and tried to get his gun away, and he was shot in the front, not in the back. Many of the witnesses who claimed to see Brown running away were actually reporting a story they heard that he was running, and they did not actually see what happened themselves.

In the Garner case, a Staten Island grand jury decided not to indict any of the arresting officers involved in Gardner's death in police custody. Despite Garner's pleas that "I can't breathe" in his final moments, he was continuing to struggle, and in New York, chokeholds aren't illegal under state law when used by a cop during a lawful arrest. Even though Garner was only selling untaxed cigarettes on the street, he was committing a crime, providing a legal basis for his arrest. Unfortunately, for Garner, he was suffering from a number of medical ailments, including advanced diabetes, heart disease, and a severe case of asthma that could have easily killed him when he was subjected to what otherwise would have been an ordinary chokehold, as described in a *New York Post* article on how Garner was a victim of his own doing due to resisting arrest.[13]

---

[13] Bob McManus, "Blame Only the Man Who Decided Tragically to Resist," *New York Post,* December 4, 2016. http://nypost.com/2014/12/04/eric-garner-was-a-victim-of-himself-for-deciding-to-resist

The Civil Litigation

Finally, whatever the outcome of a criminal investigation or in a trial, if one occurs, the officer in a fatal shooting can still be subjected to a civil lawsuit. It does not matter if the officer is found not guilty in a criminal trial, he still could be found responsible in a civil suit, because this has a lower burden of proof (where a preponderance of the evidence is required to find the defendant liable) than in a criminal justice hearing (where a certainty of a doubt is required to find criminal responsibility). Moreover, in the civil suit, the jurors can be swayed by outside social and media pressure, even if they are supposed to judge the evidence objectively. As a result, they may be influenced by their emotions or by popular opinion, and they may judge the officer to be at fault, despite what the evidence may show.

The High Financial and Psychological Costs

Making matters even worse for the officer is the financial burden resulting from any criminal or civil trial. While the city or county with jurisdiction over the incident may fund its own defense, the officer typically has to pay to defend him or herself.

Thus, he or she faces a high risk of ruinous civil damages, and even if the officer is found not liable, he or she will still have very high expenses for a defense lawyer, since a defense can cost many thousands if not hundreds of thousands of dollars. Such a high financial hit can put the officer's home and property at risk and drain any savings. Besides having to pay for any expenses for an attorney and court costs, the officer might have to additionally pay any damages assessed if he or she loses. It is no wonder that any officer normally experiences a high level of stress, often sufficient to result in PTSD (post-traumatic stress disorder) as the officer tries to pull his or her life together after a shooting incident.

Thus, as much as many citizens may think out-of-control police officers are acting out of racial bias in shooting citizens and are protected by the criminal justice system, since they are usually found not guilty, the reality is very different. Officers generally are well aware of use of force guidelines, and they have been trained to respond almost instantaneously, when they perceive a potentially deadly attack against them or a third party. They know they have to respond this way to avoid the potential death of themselves or the third party. Then, when an investigation occurs at the different levels of the criminal justice system, their response under the circumstances is carefully assessed in light of these guidelines. Thus, if they are ultimately found not guilty criminally that is because the evidence supports their response. It would seem that these four levels of adjudication provide a fair way of judging the officers, in spite of the public perception that they are being unfairly let off by the criminal justice system.

Additionally, separately from any determination by the criminal justice system, they face tremendous emotional trauma and a high level of expense. In fact, the possibility of such serious penalties for shooting a civilian could lead many officers to hold back from confronting a dangerous suspect or making an arrest, leading citizens to actually become less safe, since the criminals in such situations could escape, leaving them free to prey on other citizens again.

CHAPTER 4: THE ROLE OF THE MEDIA IN PROMOTING VIOLENCE IN POLICE FATALITIES

Today, both the traditional media and social media have been playing an influential role in fanning the flames of anger towards the police. To be sure, some police officers have been too quick to shoot or have improperly vented their hostility on a hapless suspect, such as the white Tulsa police officer Betty Shelby, who shot an unarmed black man, Terence Crutcher, who had his hands above his head by the side of his stalled SUV. She was later charged with a "heat-of-passion" manslaughter charge for acting unreasonably in overreacting to the incident. [14]

But in many other cases, the media simply get it wrong, and a false story is spread virally, such that many people think it is true. As a result, when the police officer is found not guilty based on the actual evidence in the case, people believe there was no justice, that somehow the fix was in, so the police officer was wrongly acquitted.

How the Media Can Spread a False Story

A classic example of this is what happened in the case of the shooting of Michael Brown in Ferguson, Missouri by Darren Wilson, according to Lance LoRusso, a Georgia attorney specializing in representing the police in fatal homicide cases. LoRusso is also author of *Blue News*, which describes at length some of these cases where the media got it wrong or overly sensationalized the incident, along with prescriptions on what the

---

[14] Peter Holley and Katie Zezima, "White Tulsa Officer Charged in Death of Unarmed Black Man, Freed on Bond, *The Washington Post*, September 23, 2016, https://www.washingtonpost.com/news/post-nation/wp/2016/09/22/tulsa-officer-who-fatally-shot-terrence-crutcher-charged-with-first-degree-manslaughter/?utm_term=.23e8d55b2bb1

police should do in dealing with the media to more quickly get an accurate story out about what really happened.

In the Brown case, what actually happened is that Brown tried to take away Wilson's gun, while Wilson was still seated in his patrol car, and the gun went off twice – one time into Brown's finger, a second time into the door. Witnesses said that Brown was running away and was shot in the back, but their narrative was later discredited by evidence from the medical examiner that showed he wasn't shot in the back.

At the time, it was already fairly dark, and no one had their cell phones out to take pictures of the incident as it occurred. Nevertheless, the false narrative went out that Brown was shot in the back while running away, and several witnesses who weren't there made claims that they saw what happened. But in fact, no one saw the whole incident, and the false narrative was spread through social media and that became the story which was picked up by the mainstream media. Meanwhile, the police delayed in releasing their own evidence-based version of the story for five days, since they were trying to vet the initial information they received. However, by then, the false narrative had gained traction, so the later release of contradictory information by the police was viewed as part of a cover-up to protect Wilson.

Unfortunately, in such cases, the media play a major role in giving legitimacy to a false story, which only furthers its spread and general acceptance, and a subsequent correction several days later generally gets lost in the emphasis on the latest and breaking news in each day's news cycle – or it is viewed as a false whitewash. The media are on to the next big story, so attempts to correct the record get lost.

How the Police Should Respond to False Information

That's why LoRusso recommends that the police should get out the accurate information about a case much more quickly. A key reason for this recommendation is due to the tension between the police and media over the timeframe for releasing information to the public. The media want to put out the information immediately, while the police have traditionally sought to conduct a careful examination of the evidence to be sure whatever they report is accurate, and they want to protect their innocent until proven guilty. Since the police are unable to slow down the media, LoRusso suggests that the police must speed up releasing their information.

Additionally, LoRusso recommends that the police need to improve their relationships with the media, so they can become involved in commenting on any breaking news story much more quickly. As LoRusso writes in *Blue News,* a local story about a fatality by the police, which he calls a "critical incident," can quickly blossom into a major national or international news story that can become the narrative, even if inaccurate. As he explains:

> "The critical incident is also different for the media outlets. Most often, news events are covered by local media outlets. If the story gains traction beyond the borders of a metro area or a state, local affiliates or local journalists will feed the news to larger networks…
>
> While the involvement of the AP (Associated Press) may mean that the agency will be dealing with professional journalists, it also signals to law enforcement officers and agencies that the critical incident you are dealing with right now just garnered national attention. This brings a new level of scrutiny and pressure to release information…
>
> Once news coverage reaches those levels, the stories seem to take on lives of their own. The news hits a twenty-four-hour news cycle…the requests for information become fluid and endless, and the resources of the law enforcement agency

become overwhelmed, often without a clear plan to handle the situation."[15]

Balancing Out What's True and False

Certainly, this is not to say that some more sober news articles and investigative pieces don't get it right. For example, LoRusso points out that a *U.S. News and World Report* article describes how about 99.1% of all use of force incidents are appropriate, and only about 0.9% of all complaints are cleared by sanctions, which helps to put the problem of citizen deaths by police into context. Such sanctions might include suspensions or criminal charges against the officer.

However, the average citizen is not influenced as much by these actual statistics as by the sensationalized news coverage in response to individual critical incidents. This coverage plays up the violence and makes it seem that the police are at fault in most of these cases. But, in fact, the question of police fault is only raised in the very small percentage of cases that are blown up from locally covered stories into national and international news.

---

[15] LoRusso, *Blue News,* pp. 5-9.

Then, too, this focus on certain stories makes it seem that the killings of black Americans by cops is much more common than it is, while ignoring a broader truth that most killings of blacks are due to killings by other blacks, usually by guns, as also described in my book *The Price of Justice in America*.

For example, according to LoRusso, citing a University of Toledo study on the killings by police officers between 2009 and 2012, there were a total of 56,259 homicides in the U.S., according to the Uniform Crime Reports published annually by the Federal government. Out of these totals, 1491 were due to the police use of force, while 52,893 were criminal homicides or murders, which works out to about 372 persons killed by the police each year compared to about 14,065 homicides yearly. However, this number of 372 police homicides is far less than the causes of other deaths – 35,900 people killed each year in motor vehicle accidents, 38,364 persons committing suicide.

That means that people are 103 times more likely to commit suicide, 97 times more likely to be killed in a vehicle crash, and 34 times more likely to be murdered by a criminal.[16] But the media play up the individual incidents of police and citizen homicide, and the bigger picture gets lost.

The Killings of Black Males and the Police

It is also instructive to look at the relationship between the killings of black males by the police and the police killings of members of other groups to show how the media make it seem like these deaths of black males at the hands of the police are much more common than they are. For example, of the 1491 people that died from the police use of force from 2009 to 2012, 915 or 62.4% were white males, while only 481 or 32.2% were black males, and 48 or 3.2% were males of other races. Thus, the police killed more

---

[16]Richard Johnson, "Examining the Prevalence of Deaths from the Police Use of Force," Criminal Justice Program, University of Toledo, December 26, 2014. http://www.slideshare.net/robertsearfoss33/police-lethal-forcepresentation

white males than black males, even though the media make it seem like there is a police vendetta against black males. Still, 32% is more than double the 13% of the population that is black.

More significantly, the statistics show that black males were much more likely to be killed by other citizens, and in particular by black males, than by the police. During this same 2009 to 2012 time period, of the 56,259 homicide during this time, 19,000 or 33.8% were killings of black males. However, only 481 or 2.5% of these killings were due to the police use of force. By contrast, substantially more – 648 or 3.4% -- were due to justified homicides by private citizens acting in self-defense, and 17,719 or 93.3% were criminal homicides by private citizens. So private citizens killed more black males than police in both justifiable and criminal homicides.

At the same time, the vast majority of these killings in both justifiable and criminal homicides were by blacks killing blacks. While only 6% of the U.S. population is black and male, 57.9% of the individuals killed in self-defense by a private citizen were black males, and 73.1% of the black males killed under these circumstances were killed by a black citizen.

The stats also show in other ways that the major source of violence is blacks killing other blacks, rather than blacks killing or being killed by the police. For example, 90% of the black males killed in a criminal homicide were killed by another black male, whereas only 41% of the police officers killed in the line of duty were killed by black males. It is also telling that black males are 35 times more likely to be killed in a criminal homicide and equally likely to be killed in self-defense by a black citizen as they are to be killed by the police. Such statistical findings have led researchers to conclude that there is actually "significant restraint on the part of police officers nationwide in using deadly force, not an epidemic of police-initiated killings in the U.S."[17]

---

[17]Ibid.

So why is there a false perception of widespread police killings? A key reason is the role of social media and traditional media in playing up some of the killings by the police and turning them into international stories. In turn, many activist groups, such as the Black Lives Matter movement, have played up these killings, resulting in still more media coverage. By contrast, the real story should be the high level of black on black killings, which is due, as LoRusso notes, to black involvement in a high level of violent activity. Even the Toledo study points to the "heartbreaking reality of the high suicide and violent crime rates among African-American males in impoverished urban areas," a point also made in *The Price of Justice in America.*

How to Correct the Misperceptions

Under the circumstances, what can be done to correct these misperceptions fanned by the media, as well as by the activists who are ready to blame the police rather than recognize the actual reality? According to LoRusso:

> "Law enforcement needs to tell the story. They should hold press conferences when there is a police fatality incident and they should give out

information about any arrest in the case. They also need to correct perceptions. For example, in the Brown case, law enforcement was blamed for leaving Brown's body in the street for several hours. But in fact law enforcement is not permitted to move a body without the permission of the coroner...So law enforcement needs to quickly respond and correct any misunderstandings and misperceptions, because once bad news is out there, it stay there. Law enforcement needs to talk to the media more."

In sum, much of the misperception about the guilt of the police in most of these "use of force" fatality cases is due to the media not having the correct information in the first place and then spreading inaccurate stories that fuel hostility toward the police. This results in a belief in a failure of justice, when police officers are found not guilty or innocent in most of these cases, as they should be when the evidence is viewed dispassionately by judges and jurors. Unfortunately, much of this misinformation gets spread as a result of the vacuum that often occurs in the hours or days after the incident, so false stories get out in the news. Once that happens, it becomes difficult to correct this false narrative.

Therefore, law enforcement officials have to act more quickly to get out a correct version of what really happened. Certainly, they don't want to interfere with an investigation into the crime and the collection of evidence and testimony by witnesses. But as soon as they can, police officials need to put out the available information which they can release to the media. Or if necessary, with improved relationships with the media, these officials might be better able to get the media to publish the correct information and quickly correct or not publish inaccurate news. At the same time, the officials need to take care not to release information that might jeopardize the investigation while law enforcement is still gathering evidence of what really happened in the case.

ABOUT THE AUTHOR

Paul Brakke is a scientist based in the Little Rock, Arkansas area. He became interested in studying the criminal justice system when his life was turned upside down after his wife was falsely accused of aggravated assault for trying to run some kids over with her car, since the kids and some neighbors wanted her out of the neighborhood. Eventually, they had to move, as part of a plea agreement, since otherwise, Brakke's wife faced a possible 16 year jail sentence if the case went to trial and she lost. He has previously told his wife's story in *American Justice?*, along with a critique of the criminal justice system. That book's website is at www.americanjusticethebook.com.

AMERICAN JUSTICE?
Little Rock, AR 72212
(501) 707-8352
brakkep@gmail.com

www.ingramcontent.com/pod-product-compliance
Lightning Source LLC
Chambersburg PA
CBHW070037040426
42333CB00040B/1703